JOHN THOMPSON'S
EASIEST PIANO COU

FIRST CLASSICS

CW00495090

Contents

Teachers and Parents

This collection of popular classics is intended as supplementary material for those working through John Thompson's Easiest Piano Course Parts 2 and 3, taking the player up to Part 4. The pieces may also be used for sight reading practice by more advanced students.

The material is graded, and has been specifically written to tie in with the program of learning as laid out in the Course books. Dynamics, phrasing and tempo indications have been deliberately omitted from the earlier pieces, since they are not introduced until Part 3 of the Easiest Piano Course, and initially the student's attention should be focussed on playing notes and rhythms accurately. Outline fingering has been included, and in general the hand is assumed to remain in a five finger position until a new fingering indicates a position shift. The fingering should suit most hands, although logical alternatives are always possible.

John Thompson

Arrangements by Mary Thompson

Cover design by xheight design limited
Printed and bound in the United Kingdom by
Caligraving Limited, Thetford, Norfolk.

Exclusive distributors:
Music Sales Limited,
8/9 Frith Street, London W1V 5TZ

Order No. WMR000638

Theme from The Creation

Haydn

Practise for September

Can-Can

Offenbach

Practise for September

Theme from The Pastoral Symphony

Beethoven

Practise for 30/1/06. 6/2/06.

Minuet In G

Bach

Sonatina

Beethoven

A Musical Joke

Mozart

Practise for 12/2/07

Spring from The Four Seasons

Vivaldi

Morning from Peer Gynt

Grieg

Sextet

Beethoven

Theme from The Surprise Symphony

Haydn

Theme from Judas Maccabeus

Handel

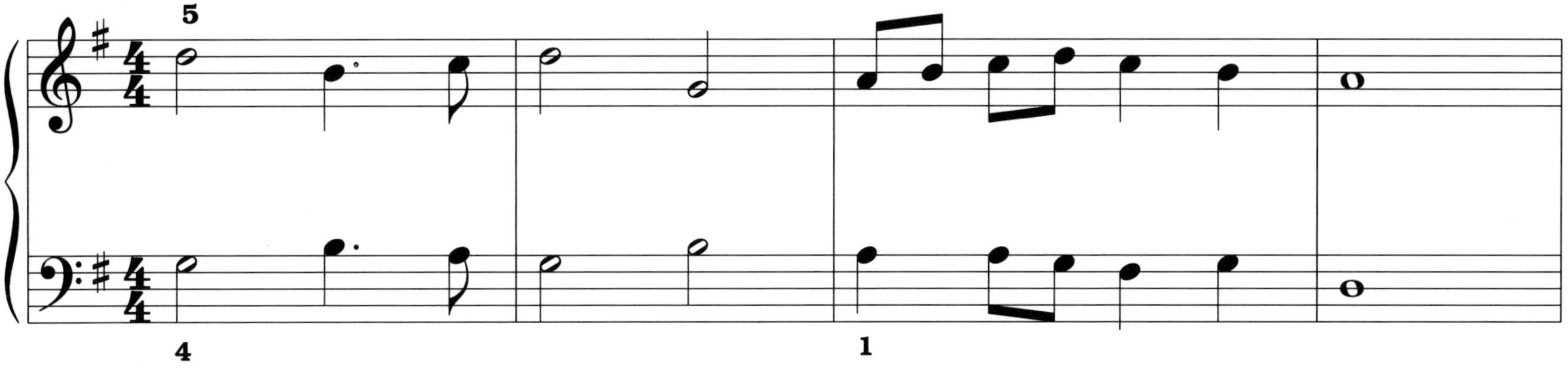

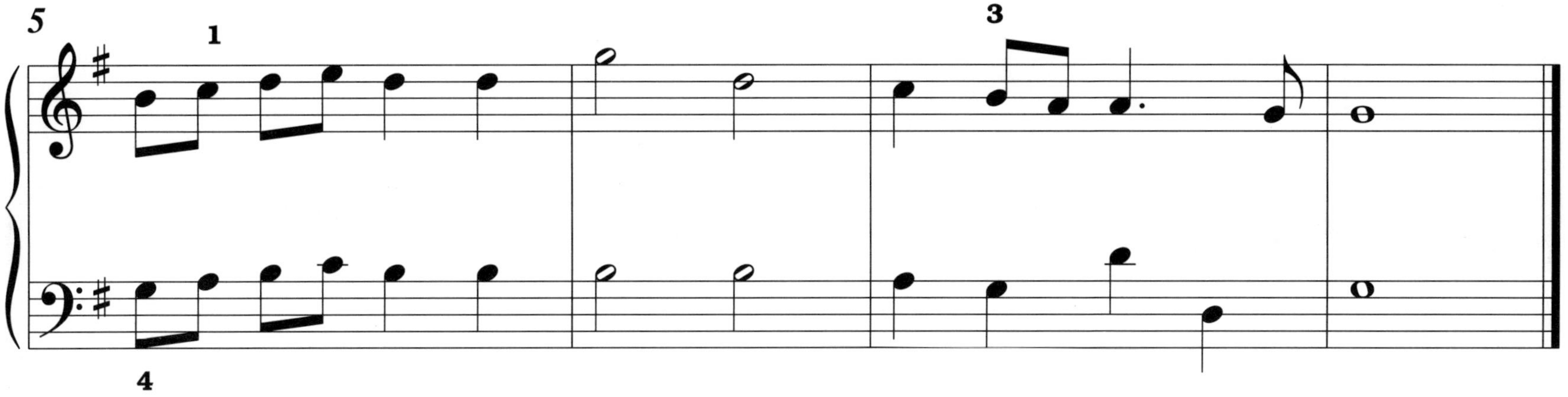

March from Carmen

Bizet

Theme from The Trout Quintet

Schubert

Waltz

Brahms

Theme from The Nutcracker

Tchaikovsky

Lullaby

Brahms

Emperor's Hymn

Moderato

Haydn

Theme from Symphony No. 7

Andante

Beethoven

Theme from Sleeping Beauty

Allegretto

Tchaikovsky

Theme from Clarinet Concerto

Nocturne Op.9, No.2

Moderato

Chopin

Bourrée from Music For The Royal Fireworks

Allegro

Handel

Theme from Swan Lake

Andante

Tchaikovsky

Romance from Eine Kleine Nachtmusik

Moderato

Mozart

Musette

Allegretto

Bach

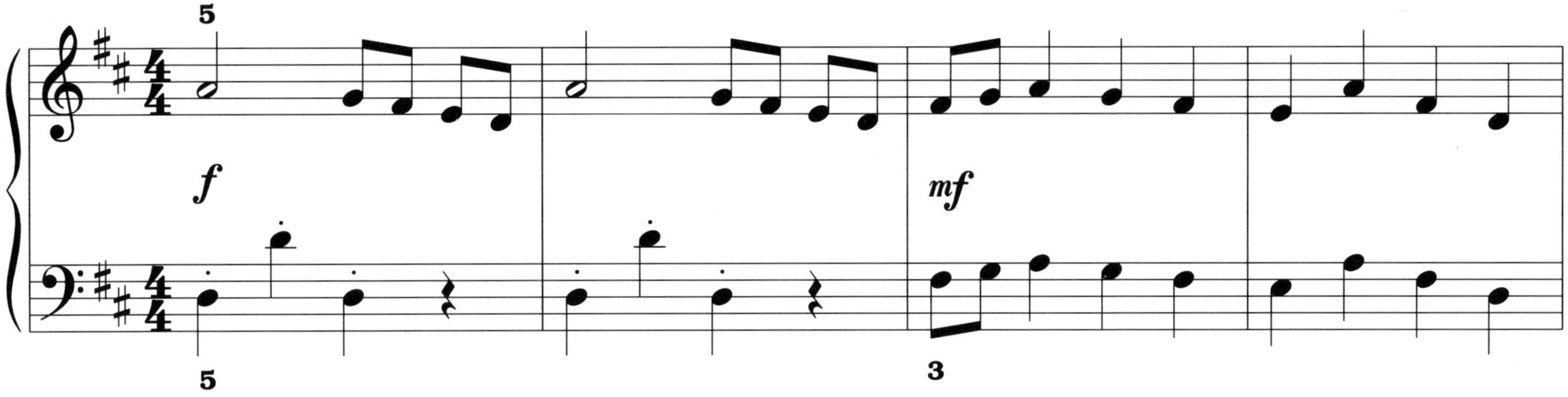

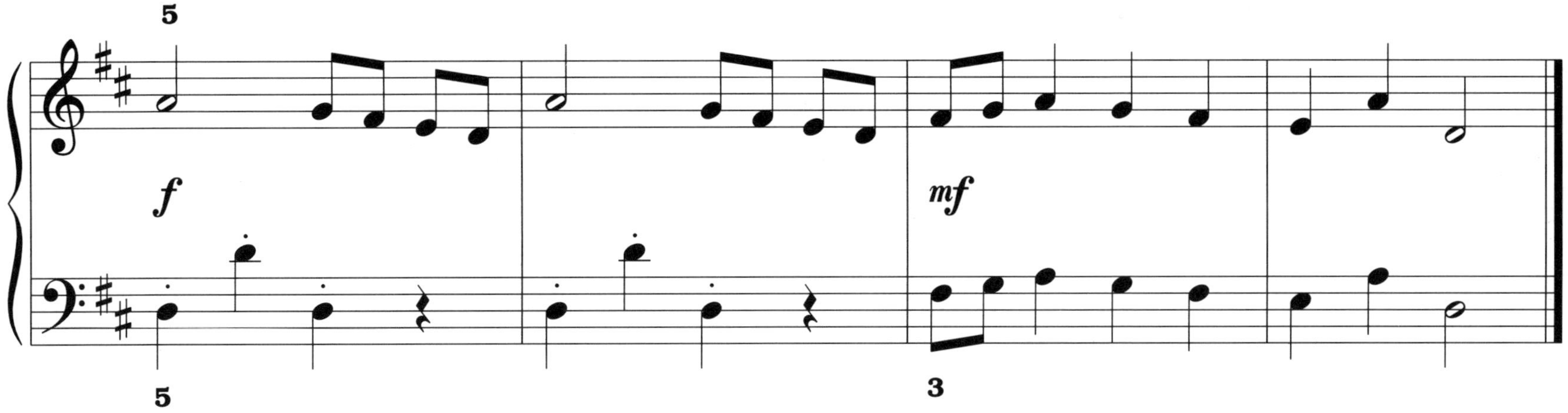

Alla Danza
from The Water Music

Moderato

Handel

17
mp
3
3
22
f
27

German Dance

Allegretto

Mozart

To A Wild Rose

Andante

MacDowell

Là Ci Darem La Mano

Allegretto

Mozart

1/03 (46282)